1 TIMOTHY

A STRONG MAN IS COURAGEOUS

1 TIMOTHY

A STRONG MAN IS COURAGEOUS

A 30-DAY DEVOTIONAL

VINCE MILLER

DAVID C COOK

transforming lives together

1 TIMOTHY
Published by David C Cook
4050 Lee Vance Drive
Colorado Springs, CO 80918 U.S.A.

Integrity Music Limited, a Division of David C Cook
Brighton, East Sussex BN1 2RE, England

DAVID C COOK® and related marks are registered trademarks of David C Cook.

The website addresses recommended throughout this book are offered as a
resource to you. These websites are not intended in any way to be or imply an
endorsement on the part of David C Cook, nor do we vouch for their content.

All Scripture quotations are taken from the ESV® Bible (The Holy Bible,
English Standard Version®), copyright © 2001 by Crossway, a publishing
ministry of Good News Publishers. Used by permission. All rights reserved.
The author has added italics to Scripture quotations for emphasis.

Library of Congress Control Number 2024930363
ISBN 978-0-8307-8623-7
eISBN 978-0-8307-8626-8

The Team: Luke McKinnon, Jeff Gerke, Jack Campbell, Karen Sherry
Cover Design: James Hershberger

Printed in Canada
First Edition 2024

1 2 3 4 5 6 7 8 9 10

012224

CONTENTS

About Vince Miller 9

Introduction 11

Identity Commanded 13

Who's Under Your Wing? 17

Stay a Little Longer 21

Don't Fall for Unbiblical Speculation. 24

It's All about the Motivation 29

What Are Your Liabilities? 32

The Race to Grace 36

Proclamations That Get Men Killed 39

Charged and Recharged 43

The Uprising and Revolt 47

Tell Them Why. 51

You Have to Want to Lead 54

No Unbiblical Idea Will Ever Outlast the Truth 58

When Worship Music Ain't Worship 62

Faithful Men Oppose Deceit. 66

It's Time to Move from Learner to Leader 70

What Is Spiritual Training? 74

Jesus, the Ultimate Deadlifter 78

Do You Want to Experience Supernatural Power? 81

Be a Watcher 85

See Believers as Family 89

Muzzle Once or Honor Twice 93

Working for Believing and Unbelieving Bosses 96

Three Signs of Inaccurate Teachers 100

The Problem of Positive Gains 104

Diverting the Deadly Progression of Sin 107

Six High-Speed Pursuits of Godly Men 111

Live It Out 115

A Covenant between Men 118

Ascend to New Heights with God 121

To every man looking for a great mentor.
The apostle Paul was one of the best.
Learn from him. And be courageous.

ABOUT VINCE MILLER

Vince Miller was born in Vallejo, California, and grew up on the West Coast. At twenty, he made a profession of faith while in college and felt a strong, sudden call to work in full-time ministry. After college and graduate school, he invested two decades working with notable ministries like Young Life and InterVarsity Christian Fellowship, as well as in the local church and in senior interim roles. He currently lives in St. Paul, Minnesota, with his wife, Christina, and their three teenage children.

In March 2014, he founded Resolute out of his passion for discipleship and leadership development of men. This passion was born out of his personal need for growth. Vince turned everywhere to find a man who would mentor, disciple, and develop him throughout his spiritual life. He often received one of two answers from well-meaning Christian leaders: *either they did not know what to do in a mentoring relationship or they simply did not have the time to do it.*

Vince soon learned that he was not alone. Many Christian men were seeking this type of mentoring relationship. Therefore, he felt compelled to build an organization that would focus on two things: ensuring that men who want to be discipled have the opportunity and giving them real tools with which to disciple other men.

Vince is known as an authentic and transparent leader who loves to communicate with men and who has a deep passion for God's Word. He has authored several books, and he is the primary creator of all Resolute content and training materials.

INTRODUCTION

Timothy was a young man known for being timid. But 1 Timothy is a letter from his mentor that would help him turn a corner. Encouraged and mentored by the great apostle Paul in this letter, Timothy would experience the leadership challenge of his life.

Back in the first century AD, Timothy served as pastor in the metropolis of Ephesus, where Paul had planted a church years before. Due to unbiblical ideologies and practices that had infiltrated the church, this congregation was now in doctrinal and organizational disrepair. And Paul, who could not travel there in person, wanted Timothy to get the church back on track. This meant Timothy would have to ask some powerful people to step down and to call some new, qualified leaders to step up. It also meant directing people back to the truth by dispelling bad doctrine and returning to the sound teaching of Jesus.

This was an unbelievable challenge for a young leader. As you will see, Paul pushed Timothy to engage. This letter is that undeniable push and clarity about what to do.

The book of 1 Timothy brings into focus the importance of mentors and the critical nature of faithful discipleship. I hope, as you read these devotions, that you will be convinced to do the same—and to mentor or be mentored in the gospel by those around you who follow Jesus. We need to be actively engaged in mentorship and discipleship in our homes, workplaces, and churches. Without this, the church in Ephesus would've been lost, and so would the church today.

We live in a day when it is critical that we disciple the next genera-
tion. So be mentored and mentor others. And in the words of Paul, "Fight
the good fight of the faith."

IDENTITY COMMANDED

"Paul, an apostle of Christ Jesus by command of
God our Savior and of Christ Jesus our hope."

1 Timothy 1:1

Who was Paul?

Paul was a man who used to be known as Saul. In the book of Acts, we discover that Saul was a high-ranking, wealthy, and well-educated Jewish man, a Pharisee, and one of the most vigorous opponents of Jesus and his followers. History tells us that Saul was so adamantly opposed to believers in Jesus and his resurrection that he found ways to justify malicious imprisoning, beating, and killing of Christians.

This is a description of a strong opponent. Yet even as Saul was in the process of hunting down followers of Christ, the resurrected Jesus was planning to confront him. Because of this dramatic supernatural confrontation, Saul was radically transformed into a follower of Jesus. He would then go on to become one of history's greatest proponents of the faith. And to mark this change in himself, he took a different name—Paul.

In fact, his transformation was so radical that his former allies, the Jewish religious leaders, had a hard time believing it—and so did his new

Christian allies. Paul would spend years reconciling the tenets of the Jewish faith with the issues that arose from his newfound belief and identity in Jesus.

One of the great challenges Christian men encounter is knowing how to live out their identity in Jesus Christ. It was true in Paul's time, and it's just as true in ours. While Christians in the West have seen gains in some areas, we've also experienced setbacks. Humans tend to come up with endless ways to throw off authority, especially God's. People on all parts of the political spectrum are feeling threatened. And this affects how we talk about, live out, and find our way to knowing our identity in Christ.

But as Paul said in another letter:

I am not ashamed of the gospel, for it is the power of God for salvation to everyone who believes. (Rom. 1:16)

This was an important declaration by Paul regarding what he believed about himself and why he was doing it. He opened 1 Timothy with a similar declaration—not just a casual salutation but a statement about who Paul was as declared by God himself. Paul stated he was a messenger of Jesus by command of the most high God.

Remember, brother, that God finds no shame in you. Jesus bore your shame on the cross. No Christian should be ashamed of who he is and what he believes. It makes no difference what others say about you, what you say about yourself, or even what your past says about you. The only thing that matters is what God says about you. He is the one who makes men and remakes their identity. He can take opponents—like you have been at some point in your life—and reshape them into the greatest of *proponents*. Live in this identity today regardless of what comes your way, because the only identity that matters is the one God has given you.

The only thing that matters is what God says about you.

ASK THIS

Are you living in the truth of your identity in Christ or the shame that the world projects onto you?

DO THIS

Live unashamed in his identity.

PRAY THIS

God, I believe you bore all my shame, and I choose to be confident in the work and identity you have given me.

JOURNAL

IDENTITY COMMANDED

WHO'S UNDER YOUR WING?

"To Timothy, my true child in the faith: Grace,
mercy, and peace from God the Father and
Christ Jesus our Lord."

1 Timothy 1:2

Paul wrote this letter to a young man named Timothy. They had met on Paul's second missionary journey when he passed through a town called Lystra in modern-day Turkey.

On Paul's previous missionary journey, he had preached in Lystra and converted a few followers. But Jewish zealots from towns he had already preached in chased him down, beat him close to death, and dragged him out of the city, assuming he was dead. But he survived. And instead of leaving, Paul went right back into the city and kept preaching.

On his second trip, he stopped at Lystra again, and it was on this trip that he met Timothy. At the time, Timothy was living with his mother and grandmother. There is no mention of his father in 2 Timothy 1, leading scholars to assume that his father had died. We discover that Timothy's mother was Jewish and a new follower of Jesus, maybe a disciple who had come to faith as a result of Paul's first trip.

Paul decided he was going to bring Timothy along on his travels. He took Timothy under his wing like he would a son, developing him as a key leader in the early church.

If you have been a follower of Jesus for a while and you don't currently have a young man "under your wing," this greeting from Paul to Timothy might encourage you to start looking for one. Even the great apostle Paul had someone he was actively mentoring.

In 1 Timothy, we'll listen to Paul actively mentoring Timothy. This letter is not just about cleaning up bad doctrine in a church. It's also a letter from an older man directing a younger man on how to lead through a very challenging situation. Today, more than ever, we need older men showing younger men how to do this.

I want you to pray a simple prayer. If you are a young man in life or the faith, I want you to pray that God will bring a wiser man like Paul across your path today. And if you are an older man, I want you to pray that God will bring a young man across your path today. After you pray, I want you to look up and anticipate that God will do just that. Let's see what God does.

We need older men showing younger men how to lead through challenging situations.

ASK THIS

Do you need a younger or older man in your life today?

DO THIS

Pray for one and then anticipate God's answer. If you already have this connection, then get ready to see how Paul and Timothy learned from each other.

PRAY THIS

God, bring a man across my path today who will help me grow as a man and leader.

JOURNAL

WHO'S UNDER YOUR WING?

_____

_____

_____

_____

_____

_____

_____

_____

_____

_____

_____

_____

_____

_____

_____

_____

_____

_____

_____

_____

_____

_____

_____

_____

_____

_____

_____

STAY A LITTLE LONGER

"As I urged you when I was going to Macedonia,
remain at Ephesus so that you may charge certain
persons not to teach any different doctrine."

1 Timothy 1:3

The word *urged* had a special emphasis for Paul. Timothy, his young protégé, was sometimes known for being a little timid. Since Paul would not be able to get to Ephesus himself, he urged Timothy to stay because Ephesus was a crucial city for expanding the gospel. But this meant that Timothy would have to lean into some hard work.

I don't know about you, but there have been times when I have not wanted to do some challenging things that might involve conflict. I'm not a guy who likes confrontation, but by leaning into disputes and sticking with them, I have learned some measures for moving through them.

Paul was a master at handling conflict. In the New Testament, you will not find a man with thicker skin and more resolve when it comes to conflict. He was beaten, stoned, rejected, condemned, and imprisoned for his faith. But he was also well educated and skilled at public debate.

Timothy, on the other hand, was very different. He was raised by his mother, not as well educated, new to his faith, and young. He was also much younger, less educated, and less known than many of the people he would be confronting in the church in Ephesus.

And still, Paul pushed him to lean into this opportunity, do the hard thing, and "remain at Ephesus."

Sometimes we need a little push in our spiritual life. We need someone to tell us, "Stay a little longer." So today, that's my word to you. I want to challenge you to remain at Ephesus. Stay in the fight for your marriage a little longer. Battle it out one more day with that repetitive sin. Keep sharing your faith with a disobedient or wayward child. Keep believing that God will save that friend, relative, and neighbor. Don't give up just yet. You might discover there is something God wants to do for you in the staying that you'll only learn by doing the hard thing one more day.

Keep believing that God will save that friend, relative, and neighbor.

ASK THIS

What is the hard thing you need to do one more day?

DO THIS

Tell God what makes it hard. He will listen.

PRAY THIS

God, give me the strength to do the hard thing I don't feel like doing today.

JOURNAL

STAY A LITTLE LONGER

DON'T FALL FOR UNBIBLICAL SPECULATION

"Remain at Ephesus so that you may charge
certain persons not to teach any different doctrine,
nor to devote themselves to myths and endless
genealogies, which promote speculations rather
than the stewardship from God that is by faith."

1 Timothy 1:3–4

In the previous devotion, we saw that Paul urged Timothy, his young disciple, to stay in Ephesus. He needed to *stay* because the church at Ephesus was getting some false teaching. And Timothy needed the *urging* because he was known for being timid.

The metropolis in any area of the world has always been the epicenter for sharing new ideas. That was why Paul spent time both in small towns and in major cities. Ancient Ephesus was a coastal city with as many as 250,000 residents. Because it was a major port, it was always full of activity. Some of the wealthiest people in the ancient world lived on the hillside of trendy Ephesus, giving them a breathtaking view. The city had a modern water system, modern businesses, and a large modern theater (which still exists today) that held about 25,000 people.

Paul was personally familiar with how large and dangerous Ephesus could be. Before he wrote this letter to Timothy, when he'd spent a long time in the city, his preaching had resulted in a major riot that came to a head in that theater.

One of the primary issues for Christians at Ephesus was the constant development of new ideologies. Because Ephesus was both a port and a center for philosophical thinking in the Roman Empire, new ideas were always on the rise there. We have seen this happen all across history, right up to today. And the unbiblical ideologies in their day threatened the gospel just as much as the unbiblical ideologies in our day do.

This was the reason Paul wrote the letter. He had heard that unbiblical ideologies had infiltrated the church, and some influential people were mixing these ideas, concepts, and beliefs with the gospel's truth.

But notice in the text that Paul said these ideas "promote speculations." For me, this signaled the reason for the issues at Ephesus. Paul was warning Timothy that he had heard believers were embracing new ideas and that they were speculating on them for too long. These speculations had now captured their attention, like a magic trick or sleight of hand. And like a magic trick, these ideas had shreds of truth that concealed something hidden—a falsehood or lie (which was the trick). But by the time they figured out the trick or the lie, they would have speculated too long. Thus, the idea had been embraced to the point that it was being supported and taught to others.

I don't think I need to make a specific contemporary connection, but this is happening in our corporations, schools, and even some churches today. And by the time we realize what is going on, the ideology is seeded too deep, and returning to the truth becomes challenging.

Guess what? Paul wanted Timothy to deal with it. To address unbiblical speculation in the church.

This is why we need to be reading God's Word personally, for ourselves. We cannot sit back and accept what we're being taught. We need to test everything, even things taught by Christian leaders. We need to read God's Word, study it, and test all new ideologies against it.

We need to be reading God's Word for ourselves. We cannot sit back and accept what we're being taught.

If we don't, we might drift and discover we no longer follow God because we've been following man-made speculations with only shreds of truth. So the next time you find that you or your church is speculating, stop speculating and start searching. Truth is found by searching for the truth in the Truth, not by speculating about it.

ASK THIS

What one unbiblical ideology are you most concerned about today?

DO THIS

Search God's Word for a response to that ideology.

PRAY THIS

God, give me the wisdom to discern truth and avoid meaningless speculation.

JOURNAL

DON'T FALL FOR UNBIBLICAL SPECULATION

_____

_____

_____

_____

_____

_____

_____

_____

_____

_____

_____

_____

_____

_____

_____

_____

_____

_____

_____

_____

_____

_____

_____

IT'S ALL ABOUT THE MOTIVATION

"The aim of our charge is love that issues from a pure heart and a good conscience and a sincere faith. Certain persons, by swerving from these, have wandered away into vain discussion, desiring to be teachers of the law, without understanding either what they are saying or the things about which they make confident assertions."

1 Timothy 1:5–7

In the first few verses, we learn that Paul wanted Timothy to stay in Ephesus. Paul knew that Timothy was ideal for handling this situation because he was pure of heart, had a good conscience, and was sincere in his faith. This was everything Paul wanted the believers in Ephesus to be, and he knew that if Timothy stayed, they would see this in how Timothy lived and approached his faith and ministry. But this would be in sharp contrast to "certain believers" in Ephesus, whose motivations were public, showy, and assertive.

This can easily happen to any believer in a position of leadership. We get a little intoxicated with the power of our position or the pedestal we lead from, and gradually our motivation shifts. We leave the motivation from a pure heart and become attracted to the power of publicity done for our own advantage. We have seen this happen to professionals and pastors in our time. And that's what happened in Ephesus in Paul's day.

Today, I want to encourage you to assess your motivation. Evaluate it against the plumb line Paul gave Timothy: love that comes from a pure heart, a good conscience, and a sincere faith. If there is something you are about to do today that does not line up with this, then ask this question, "What's my real motivation?" And then, I would plumb it up before you do something public, showy, and assertive that may result in uncomfortable public correction.

"What's my real motivation?"

ASK THIS

What motivation do you need to address today?

DO THIS

Be brave and address it. Plumb it up before it's too late.

PRAY THIS

God, plumb up my motivation to your will.

JOURNAL

IT'S ALL ABOUT THE MOTIVATION

WHAT ARE YOUR LIABILITIES?

"I thank him who has given me strength, Christ Jesus
our Lord, because he judged me faithful, appointing
me to his service, though formerly I was a blasphemer,
persecutor, and insolent opponent. But I received
mercy because I had acted ignorantly in unbelief, and
the grace of our Lord overflowed for me with the faith
and love that are in Christ Jesus."

1 Timothy 1:12–14

In this next section, Paul centered on himself, but not in a self-centered way. Rather, he illustrated how Christ redeemed him out of his malice toward Christians and how Christ wanted to use Timothy to do this same work with false teachers in Ephesus. Paul declared that he too was once like these Ephesians—a hater, a bully, and a brazen man.

I love that Paul could list his liabilities: "blasphemer, persecutor, and insolent opponent." Not every man is able to admit his failures. But I also love that he saw these attributes as something in the past—"though *formerly* I was a blasphemer, persecutor, and insolent opponent."

Paul did two things here that every Christian man needs to do:

1. He named his liabilities.
2. He perceived them as former.

First, we should be able to name our liabilities. Some men cannot. Either they are too arrogant to admit them, they are too concerned about the changes required, or they haven't taken the time to reflect on what their liabilities might be. So, what are yours? Can you name and identify them—specifically, not just generally?

Second, if you do know your liabilities and have been humbled by them, are they becoming something of the past, or do you cling to them for some reason, maybe because you have trouble accepting God's grace?

If you find it difficult to answer these questions, do what Paul did here: name your liabilities, and then see them in the light of God's grace. Because until you do, you might be just as wrong as the false teachers in Ephesus: a self-sufficient man living by the law and not by grace.

Name your liabilities, and then see them in the light of God's grace.

ASK THIS

Have you done the two steps mentioned above?

DO THIS

List your liabilities, and accept God's grace again.

PRAY THIS

God, I need your grace.

JOURNAL

WHAT ARE YOUR LIABILITIES?

THE RACE TO GRACE

"The saying is trustworthy and deserving of full
acceptance, that Christ Jesus came into the world to
save sinners, of whom I am the foremost. But I received
mercy for this reason, that in me, as the foremost, Jesus
Christ might display his perfect patience as an example
to those who were to believe in him for eternal life."

1 Timothy 1:15–16

The first part of this "power text" perfectly captures how some men feel in their relationship with God. We feel very far from God because of our sins, and we tend to fixate on this.

It's true that we should know, identify, and accept the full weight of our sins. If we don't, we won't experience the other side of what Paul declared here. Because he focused not only on how great his sin was but also on the mercy of Jesus. He realized that while he could spend his life fixating on his sins, there was something better to fix his mind on: the patience and mercy of Jesus considering his great sin. By accepting this mercy, living in it, and fixating on it, his salvation bore witness to all the great attributes of Christ and not just the great sin of his past.

So, if you are fixating on the sins of your past, maybe today is the day to turn that focus to Jesus's love, mercy, grace, and forgiveness. Turn your sin over to him in confession and turn to his grace. See not only your sin but also his great mercy. Instead, day after day, turn all your attention to how great Jesus's mercy is despite your sin.

> ——— Maybe today is the day to turn your focus to Jesus's love, mercy, grace, and forgiveness. ———

ASK THIS

Are you overfixated on your sin and missing God's grace?

DO THIS

Receive his grace in prayer.

PRAY THIS

God, your grace is so great. Help me to know it and receive it fully.

JOURNAL

THE RACE TO GRACE

PROCLAMATIONS THAT GET MEN KILLED

"To the King of the ages, immortal, invisible, the only
God, be honor and glory forever and ever. Amen."

1 Timothy 1:17

It's possible to read some phrases in God's Word without understanding their explosive impact. This is one of those.

Remember, this letter is from an older man named Paul and was written to Timothy, his "son in the faith." At the end of the letter's introduction, Paul dropped in this little poem. It's a description of all that God had done for him, to him, and with him. It's a declaration of who God was to Paul. God was the only King and the greatest being of all time. Many experts believe this phrase may have been a saying or axiom of the early church.

It's also what got Paul killed.

This little saying right here, the proclamation that Jesus Christ was King, would lead to Paul's second imprisonment, some of the most significant conflicts in his life—both with the government and with the church—and eventually his death.

Our present time is calling for men like Paul. Men who will stand up and speak up for what they believe. Men who are willing to live and die by the convictions they proclaim.

Don't confuse this with protesting against the church or the government. That's not what Paul did here. He wasn't living to *protest* but to *proclaim* a King who is greater than any other king. It's this proclamation that cost him his life because it implied he stood for no one and nothing else. This sort of simple proclamation also advanced the gospel message across the Roman Empire.

> Our present time is calling
> for men like Paul. Men who
> will stand up and speak up
> for what they believe.

My question for you today is this: What message has God called you to proclaim that will advance the gospel message?

ASK THIS

What message do you need to proclaim?

DO THIS

What are you waiting for? Proclaim it.

PRAY THIS

God, use the message you gave me to advance your gospel.

JOURNAL

PROCLAMATIONS THAT GET MEN KILLED

_____
_____
_____
_____
_____
_____
_____
_____
_____
_____
_____
_____
_____
_____
_____
_____
_____
_____
_____
_____
_____
_____
_____
_____

CHARGED AND RECHARGED

"This charge I entrust to you, Timothy, my child, in
accordance with the prophecies previously made about
you, that by them you may wage the good warfare,
holding faith and a good conscience."

1 Timothy 1:18–19

This passage hit me hard. I think because Paul did two things every mentor and leader needs to do.

First, he gave his protégé a charge. Do you know why? Because when someone needs direction, mere hints or suggestions don't always work. If you leave it up to a hint or a suggestion, the person on the other side will draw conclusions and assumptions about what you might want them to do. Most of the time, they'll get it wrong. Especially when it comes to things of a spiritual nature. Paul knew that Timothy had to not get this one wrong. There was too much at stake—like the gospel message to the church in Ephesus.

Second, Paul connected this charge with a reminder about some previous promises given to Timothy. This means that Paul's charge here was really a *recharge*. This recharge was just a reminder. Sometimes we need to be reminded, don't we?

Paul revealed right in this verse why he was charging and reminding Timothy. It was so Timothy would "wage the good warfare, holding faith and a good conscience." Or, in my words, Paul charged and reminded Timothy so he would never stop acting and believing as God's man.

We just looked closely at the bark on the tree. Now let's step back for a moment and look at the tree.

Here's what Paul was doing: he was repeating to Timothy something he had been told time and time again. But this time, Paul was saying it with new emphasis, because he knew it would meet with new learning.

Isn't this true for all of us? How many times have you read one text in the Bible and then read it again after you went through a challenge, difficulty, or some opposition in your life, and suddenly, you saw new meaning in it? That has happened many times in my life. And each time, it gives us a good reason to cling to the promises in God's Word. It gives us a good reason to repeat them time and time again to ourselves.

Here is one I repeat quite frequently to my family and those who listen to me: "Live all in for him who lived all in for you." Why do I repeat it? Because we all need reminders that charge and recharge us.

"Live all in for him who lived all in for you."

ASK THIS

What promise do you need to cling to today?

DO THIS

Be reminded and charged or recharged.

PRAY THIS

God, I cling to the hope and promise you have given me.

JOURNAL

CHARGED AND RECHARGED

THE UPRISING AND REVOLT

"First of all, then, I urge that supplications, prayers,
intercessions, and thanksgivings be made for all people,
for kings and all who are in high positions, that we may
lead a peaceful and quiet life, godly and dignified in every
way. This is good, and it is pleasing in the sight of God our
Savior, who desires all people to be saved and to come to
the knowledge of the truth."

1 Timothy 2:1–4

This text is an excellent reminder to us, given the times in which we live.

Here, Paul was warning Timothy that the Christian movement could easily be misinterpreted as an uprising. But that was never the goal. Paul never intended for his ministry to result in a revolt against Jews, Romans, or the government. Now Paul did preach a challenging gospel, which earned him a reputation for being a troublemaker. But a lot of the trouble around him was stirred up by other people—like angry mobs, merchants, and malicious Jews—which is exactly what happened the last time he was in Ephesus.

Paul knew better than most that preaching the gospel could have unintended effects and be interpreted as an attack on business, religion, and the government, resulting in backlash or even revolt. But right here, he cleared this up: That was not his goal. His goal was to represent Jesus honorably in hopes of presenting the gospel message to all people.

So he told Timothy to pray and intercede for everyone, especially those who led the government.

I think this call to action is spot-on for our time. We live in a day when our country is profoundly divided on just about every issue. Everything is politicized. We are in a contentious war, but ultimately it's a war against spiritual untruth. Though we do have a civic duty to speak up and stand up, we must remember that our aim is salvation for all. Our goal is that others may know his truth, not ours. We have to remember this. One of the best ways to be reminded of this goal is to pray for the lost and all those who lead in every level of our government.

Our goal is that others may know his truth, not ours.

The next time you are a little irritated by what's happening in your city, state, or country, turn this irritation into a prompt to pray for our leaders—including those you don't agree with. It might remind you to aim for the higher goal—salvation and understanding for all who are lost.

ASK THIS

Who do you disagree with that you need to be praying for?

DO THIS

Pray for them right now.

PRAY THIS

God, bring salvation to those who are lost and open their minds to the knowledge of the truth.

JOURNAL

THE UPRISING AND REVOLT

TELL THEM WHY

"This is good, and it is pleasing in the sight of God our
Savior, who desires all people to be saved and to come to
the knowledge of the truth. For there is one God, and there
is one mediator between God and men, the man Christ
Jesus, who gave himself as a ransom for all, which is the
testimony given at the proper time. For this I was appointed
a preacher and an apostle (I am telling the truth, I am not
lying), a teacher of the Gentiles in faith and truth."

1 Timothy 2:3–7

Here, Paul gave three theological reasons for why Timothy should be a godly citizen and pray for those in higher authority. First, he declared that God was the authority over all humanity. Second, he said that God gave humanity a mediator (his Son, Jesus). Third, he stated that God purchased humanity's freedom at great cost. This led to his final point: God had appointed Paul to preach about these things.

What do we learn from this passage? We learn that it is important to tell people our reasons.

I cannot count how many times while I was teaching lessons to my children they asked me *why*. Why they could or could not do something. Much of the time, I needed to give them a biblical reason for doing or not doing whatever it was. Which, by the way, is the right thing for a father, leader, husband, and man to do. When we give people scriptural reasons for doing and not doing something, it connects real-life questions to answers found in the truth. It fuses thoughts and actions with a biblical perspective and helps others see and hopefully develop a similar worldview.

It is important to tell people our reasons.

So, instead of letting people guess why you are doing or not doing something, tell them why. That's what Paul did. And this is not just another discipleship strategy. It's a means of sharing the gospel and the good news of Jesus Christ in our day-to-day behaviors.

ASK THIS

Is there someone to whom you might need to explain why?

DO THIS

Be ready to answer and tell them why.

PRAY THIS

God, give me divine knowledge so I can explain why.

JOURNAL

TELL THEM WHY

YOU HAVE TO WANT TO LEAD

"The saying is trustworthy: If anyone
aspires to the office of overseer,
he desires a noble task."

1 Timothy 3:1

At the front of Paul's mind was the leadership crisis in this church. He needed Timothy to identify leaders who were up for the job. A church without appointed leaders is left with a void that others will step into. Which is what was happening in the church at Ephesus. So, Timothy needed to find some qualified leaders, and Paul told him to start with men who aspired to lead.

I have never had the desire to be an elder in the church. I might be qualified in some senses, but I don't desire it. This is a little laughable because I have trained and discipled hundreds of men for leadership in the church. Yet, still, I don't desire it. Which means I am disqualified from this role.

Why is desire so important in this context? It's important because leadership is challenging. And when it gets challenging, you will have to lean on your desire and aspiration when it gets tough. Those qualities, those goals, will remind you why you signed up for leading—you desired it.

This is true in any leadership situation. Every form of leadership has challenging moments. In fact, let's remember that Timothy had signed up with Paul way back in Lystra. Though Timothy was a little timid, and though when he signed on he might not have understood that he would end up as a pastor in faraway Ephesus, he nevertheless had desired to join Paul in his ministry. Therefore, Paul was pushing him a bit.

Also, Paul didn't like leaders who quit when the going got tough. This was what John Mark had done on one of Paul's trips, and it had caused a split between Paul and Barnabas (Acts 15:36–39).

When leadership gets challenging, you will have to lean on your desire and aspiration.

So today, if you are in a leadership position and the going is getting tough, can I encourage you to do something? Remind yourself why you signed up to do it. Take a second to recall that moment when you were full of excitement and remember your *why*. Maybe that will give you the spiritual and emotional boost you need today to keep on keeping on.

If you aspire to do something like that, I am praying for you. Because God's church needs leaders just like you.

ASK THIS

Do you aspire and desire to lead?

DO THIS

Reflect on what form of leadership God is calling you to.

PRAY THIS

God, you are the leader, and I am the follower. If you need me to serve a group of your people as a leader, let me know.

JOURNAL

YOU HAVE TO WANT TO LEAD

NO UNBIBLICAL IDEA WILL EVER OUTLAST THE TRUTH

"I hope to come to you soon, but I am writing
these things to you so that, if I delay, you may
know how one ought to behave in the
household of God, which is the church of the
living God, a pillar and buttress of the truth."

1 Timothy 3:14–15

When I read this passage, I always wonder if I'm detecting a tone of concern in Paul. To me, he sounds worried that he was not going to be able to get to Ephesus. In light of this concern, he hoped Timothy could establish leaders of biblical character who would give the church its needed direction. Why? Because Paul heard that the church was embracing ideologies that had no biblical basis. I think we'd have to say that there is a wave of this happening in the church today.

Then Paul added a beautiful metaphor, which was a bit of a dig at these unbiblical ideologies. He described the church as a structure built by a living God on the immovable foundation and pillars of truth.

When he wrote this, I am sure Paul saw in his mind's eye the Temple of Diana. This temple was one of the most impressive structures of the time, listed as one of the seven wonders of the ancient world, and it stood right on the ridge of Ephesus. It was a temple with a massive foundation, supporting one hundred towering pillars. In the center stood a statue of the goddess Diana, the site of ritual prostitution.

In this text, Paul replaced the vivid and familiar image with another: a temple not made by human hands for a dead Goddess, but a temple built by a living God and upon the pillars and foundation of truth.

> So that, if I delay, you may know how one ought to behave in the household of God, which is the church of the living God, a pillar and buttress of the truth. (1 Tim. 3:14–15)

Do you know what we need in our churches today? We need less culture and more truth. We need less of what's current, trendy, popular, and "relevant." We need more of what's stable, unchanging, timeless, and trustworthy. But this requires men of truth, men who live by the truth, to engage and speak the truth.

We need less culture and more truth.

That's what Paul was concerned about here. Would some men step up? You know what? I want to be a man like that. I bet you do too.

The Temple of Diana is gone. It no longer exists. A storm destroyed it. That's going to be the end for every unbiblical ideology. It will last only until the next storm. But the living God and his truth will stand forever. And that's something I want to get behind.

ASK THIS

Are you getting behind the living God and his truth?

DO THIS

Get behind his truth, not the next popular and unbiblical ideology.

PRAY THIS

God, adjust my thoughts, actions, and speech to your truth.

JOURNAL

NO UNBIBLICAL IDEA WILL EVER OUTLAST THE TRUTH

WHEN WORSHIP MUSIC
AIN'T WORSHIP

"Great indeed, we confess, is the mystery of godliness:
He was manifested in the flesh, vindicated by the Spirit,
seen by angels, proclaimed among the nations, believed
on in the world, taken up in glory."

1 Timothy 3:16

I think it is super interesting that Paul used a song to address untruth. He used this song, which might've been the early church's equivalent of a worship song, to correct some wrong theology. Paul also used this song to set up an attack on false teachers, which he would bring up in chapter 4.

The reason I find this so interesting is that it seems to me that in the church today, we do the opposite. Rather than use songs to teach doctrine and worship the greatness of God, so many times we leverage music to elicit a *feeling* from people. We lead the church in worship that doesn't really worship God.

What some of these so-called worship songs do is sprinkle in bits and pieces of the truth, leaving openings for untruths that elicit feelings but don't cause people to worship God. Therefore, many of the people participating feel as if they have worshipped, but it's all based on untruth. They leave church feeling close to God, but instead, they are close only to their good feelings. What's more, they are now indoctrinated with untruths they have accepted as truth.

But not Paul. He used a hymn to teach rich theological truths about Jesus, to worship God, and to attack untruths.

So the next time you are sitting in church or listening to worship music, make sure you ask two questions about the song you are listening to:

- Who is this song to? (If it's to anyone but God, then it's not worship to God.)
- What is this song about? (If it's about anyone but God, then it's not worship about God.)

Try it this week and see.

Paul used a hymn to teach rich theological truths about Jesus, to worship God, and to attack untruths.

ASK THIS

Are you worshipping God, or are you worshipping your feelings?

DO THIS

Listen to Christian music this week and ask those two questions.

PRAY THIS

God, may my worship be about only you and nothing else.

JOURNAL

WHEN WORSHIP MUSIC AIN'T WORSHIP

FAITHFUL MEN
OPPOSE DECEIT

"Now the Spirit expressly says that in later times some
will depart from the faith by devoting themselves to
deceitful spirits and teachings of demons, through the
insincerity of liars whose consciences are seared."

1 Timothy 4:1–2

Over the last several years, numerous churchgoers have walked out of the church never to return. They have departed the faith, just like Paul mentioned here.

But to get the application, we must understand the issue that Paul was trying to combat. He'd been laying the groundwork for this since the start of his letter. Paul wanted Timothy to know that he was going to have to take a stand against spiritual forces, and he was going to need some leaders to help.

With the hymn in the previous few verses, Paul established a doctrinal basis founded on the person of Jesus from beginning to end. In these verses, he contrasted Jesus with the opposition. And he called these people insincere, hypocritical liars. Then, he took up some descriptive language, telling Timothy that they were former believers who had devoted themselves to deceitful spirits and demons and that they had become so entrenched that they refused to change.

This should be "front of mind" for every spiritual leader. The volume and intensity of lies and deceit in our world will always increase. At times, it might be so overwhelming that disengagement will seem like the only escape, and this is where leaders can become timid. Paul did not want Timothy to do that. He needed Timothy to stay in the game. He needed him to be faithful and to prepare a group of faithful men to lead the church in Ephesus.

What do you need to do? You may need to get into God's truth more consistently. You may need to find a group of men who are eager to study and search for the truth together. This may be the time for you to lead a group of men toward truth. If you feel any or all these calls to action, do something about it. The worst thing we can do in times like this is … nothing.

Don't do nothing.

This may be the time
for you to lead a group
of men toward truth.

ASK THIS

What do you need to do?

DO THIS

Take one step today and right now.

PRAY THIS

God, may my convictions become actions that bring glory to you and your name.

JOURNAL

FAITHFUL MEN OPPOSE DECEIT

IT'S TIME TO MOVE FROM LEARNER TO LEADER

"If you put these things before the brothers,
you will be a good servant of Christ Jesus,
being trained in the words of the faith and of
the good doctrine that you have followed."

1 Timothy 4:6

I love this moment in the letter because it's a little pause where an older man complimented a younger man on his leadership development. Paul told Timothy that he was proud of him. He congratulated him on two things he had done well to this point in his life. First, he received his spiritual training. Second, he had been practicing it. But then Paul hinted at the ever-important third and final step in Timothy's training. Do you see it here? It's found in the first clause of this text: "If you put these things before the brothers."

This was Paul's third charge: step into the leadership opportunity before you, Timothy. But it was conditional based on his action. He had to choose to step up, step out, and step into it. Paul was right to push him a little to do this.

All of us need time to receive spiritual training. We need time to learn the basics of the truth. We also need time for these lessons to synthesize into consistent actions in our lives. But at some point, we must move from learner to leader. There comes a time when we need to lead and step into the leadership challenge before us.

There is never a specific time frame for this transition, but as a general marker, I would say that at some point in the first five years of your spiritual walk as an adult, you need to have taken some steps toward leadership, whether that is formal or informal. Let's face it: many of us, even when we are young in our faith, were already leaders in some context. At present, each of us has some context in which we have leadership influence where we can put our biblical and spiritual learnings into action and practice leadership. But too many men put this off for too long. So today, in the spirit of Paul, let me challenge you to step up, step out, and step into it.

> There comes a time when we need to lead and step into the leadership challenge before us.

Try it: put before others some lesson God has been revealing to you that you have applied. Take it to your circle of influence (a friend, a peer, a brother, or a family member), and see if God doesn't take you one more step into your spiritual development—from a learner to a leader.

ASK THIS

What spiritual lesson will you put before others?

DO THIS

Take a step toward spiritual leadership.

PRAY THIS

God, show me the lesson and provide me with opportunity.

JOURNAL

IT'S TIME TO MOVE FROM LEARNER TO LEADER

WHAT IS SPIRITUAL TRAINING?

"Have nothing to do with irreverent, silly myths. Rather train yourself for godliness; for while bodily training is of some value, godliness is of value in every way, as it holds promise for the present life and also for the life to come."

1 Timothy 4:7-8

The principle here is simple: Wrong beliefs lead to wrong actions. Right beliefs lead to right actions. Paul exhorted Timothy to get his act together by being trained in godly beliefs that had eternal value.

What does spiritual training look like, and how do we get it? In the context of this letter, spiritual training includes:

- Reading the truth.
- Knowing the truth.
- Living the truth.

But we could also add that spiritual training includes:

- Discerning truth from untruth.
- Training others to read, know, live, and discern the truth.

Spiritual training assumes some things too. It assumes that:

- We're not being passive in our spiritual development.
- We're actively searching Scripture to find the truth.
- We're scanning our lives for beliefs we need to change.
- We're implementing these changes into our lives.
- Others are seeing the spiritual transformation in us and are being affected by it.

Are you ready to do some training in the gym? If so, implement one item from the list above.

Scan your life for beliefs you need to change.

ASK THIS

Are you ready to do some spiritual training in the gym?

DO THIS

Tell someone the step you need to implement.

PRAY THIS

God, train me.

JOURNAL

WHAT IS SPIRITUAL TRAINING?

JESUS, THE ULTIMATE
DEADLIFTER

"For to this end we toil and strive, because we have
our hope set on the living God, who is the Savior of
all people, especially of those who believe."

1 Timothy 4:10

Paul told Timothy the reason we need training. We go to the gym and engage in spiritual training not to get an emotional or mental lift or even to build spiritual muscle. The reason we train is to remind ourselves that there is a spiritual deadlifter who outlifted all of us.

Deadlifting is a form of weightlifting in which you lift the weight from the ground to thigh level using primarily your leg and hip muscles.

Jesus lifted a world weighed down by sin. Therefore, when we go to the gym, we train not to compete with one another, not to get bigger, and not for some selfish emotional or mental boost. We train, toil, and strive because it fixes our minds on the ultimate deadlifter—Jesus Christ. He alone lifted the weight we could not lift.

So get in the gym today. But do it to set your mind and hope on the ultimate deadlifter. That is the training. It's your daily reminder that you will never be able to lift what he has lifted for you and from you.

We train, toil, and strive because it fixes our minds on the ultimate deadlifter—Jesus Christ.

ASK THIS

What has Jesus lifted for you and from you?

DO THIS

Reflect on this and share it in the following journal space.

PRAY THIS

God, train me. May I fix my mind on you and everything you have lifted from my life of sin.

JOURNAL
JESUS, THE ULTIMATE DEADLIFTER

DO YOU WANT TO EXPERIENCE SUPERNATURAL POWER?

"Do not neglect the gift you have, which was given you
by prophecy when the council of elders laid their hands
on you. Practice these things, immerse yourself in them,
so that all may see your progress."

1 Timothy 4:14–15

Paul was reminding Timothy that he had a spiritual gift, one uniquely made for the challenges in the church at Ephesus. Timothy needed to remember it and lean on its spiritual power. But for this to happen, he would have to trust God by being immersed in the situation.

This is the challenge I see so many men face. They long to be used by God and to see his supernatural work, but they don't put themselves in situations where God can use them. They put themselves only in situations where they can trust the limits of their ability, finances, experience, or education to help them succeed. Therefore, this is what they get. They get the limited results of what their ability, finances, experience, and education can achieve.

But men who trust in the Spirit's work and become familiar with their supernatural gifts get results that blow through the limits of every natural possibility. They discover supernatural events happening in them and through them.

This is my hope for you, as it was Paul's hope for Timothy: I want you to know the limitless power of our mighty God working in and through you. Only one thing needs to happen for this to occur in your life: you must put yourself in a situation that is just beyond your ability, finances, experience, and education, and then you need to trust God.

Then hold on because, on the other side, God is working and waiting for you to know and discover the limitless power of the Spirit in and through you.

> **You must put yourself in a situation that is just beyond your ability, finances, experience, and education, and then you need to trust God.**

What will you do today?

ASK THIS

Where do you need to trust God today?

DO THIS

Trust the Spirit and not yourself.

PRAY THIS

God, show me the path to trusting you and unlocking my gifts to serve you and others.

JOURNAL

DO YOU WANT TO EXPERIENCE SUPERNATURAL POWER?

_____

_____

_____

_____

_____

_____

_____

_____

_____

_____

_____

_____

_____

_____

_____

_____

_____

_____

_____

_____

_____

_____

_____

_____

_____

BE A WATCHER

"Keep a close watch on yourself and on the teaching.
Persist in this, for by so doing you will save both
yourself and your hearers."

1 Timothy 4:16

There is so much to love about this book called 1 Timothy. I love it because it feels like we are reading a confidential letter written by a high-level leader to an apprentice. It gives us an inside look at both men from both angles. It models everything I think men want to be as leaders, and it highlights everything we want to experience as protégés.

But all mentors know a moment eventually comes when the apprentice must take responsibility for himself. That is the spirit of the words here. Paul told Timothy that it was time for him to "watch himself." In other words, Paul would not be around to coach, train, and redirect him. So from this moment forward, Timothy needed to keep a watchful eye on the things he was hearing and learning. He needed to be attentive. And he would have to persist with it too, because all kinds of false doctrines would arise, so he could not let down his guard.

I don't know about you, but I feel like this is exactly the time we're in. Our enemy the devil is working overtime to indoctrinate us with ideas that have tiny shreds of truth bound to all kinds of lies and lead to false doctrines that oppose the gospel. This is happening all across the political spectrum. These ideas find their way into the minds of unsuspecting people who bite on the shreds of truth and blindly get hooked by the many lies that lead them down a road of confusion. Many today are being led into error because of it.

But, as Paul said here, we bear a responsibility for this. An individual responsibility. As godly men, we are called to steward the truth. The first way we steward it is by "watching ourselves." By watching what we consume in thought and thus believe. Therefore, we must test every ideology against biblical truth. This is a spiritual leader's work. We must get in the gym and train our minds daily with gospel truth.

At the same time, we must "persist with it," meaning we must read, preach, and teach the truth, persisting with it even when other ideologies seem to gain traction. And we can't quit and give in, because there is hope. Hope that our truthful persistence will persuade some to salvation.

So don't quit today. You may feel alone in the battle for knowing and living the truth. But persistence with the truth may result in the salvation of someone you know and love.

We must test every ideology against biblical truth.

ASK THIS

What truth do you need to persist with, and who could it affect?

DO THIS

Name them in the following journal space.

PRAY THIS

God, may your Spirit be stronger in me than my desire to do things alone.

JOURNAL

BE A WATCHER

SEE BELIEVERS AS FAMILY

"Do not rebuke an older man but encourage him as you
would a father, younger men as brothers, older women
as mothers, younger women as sisters, in all purity."

1 Timothy 5:1–2

Based on everything we have read over the last four chapters of this book
of the Bible, we know that Timothy would have to lead through some
tough stuff. Paul knew he would have to tell some people to step up and
others to step down. How he would handle this was important. He
needed to be diplomatic. So Paul painted a picture of how he wanted
Timothy to relate to them. He encouraged him to treat them as members
of a spiritual family.

I think the modern church fails to embrace this concept. In our
time, we have reduced the church to an event we attend every week, and
therefore, it has become a mere transaction. Churchgoers are reduced to
titles with transactional meaning: attendees, consumers, and participants. But we aren't attendees, consumers, and participants—we are a
spiritual family with obligations to one another. We are members of a
family joined together by a Father through the sacrifice of his Son, and
that makes us brothers and sisters.

This spiritual family bears a weight of responsibility that requires us to treat one another as family. This means that leaders in the church need to remember that while they will have to address hard things sometimes, they are stewards of God's family. They are not leaders of an organization that drives a vision and makes decisions in a way that dismisses its family members.

This is what I have loved about learning to lead as a father. As a father, I am forced to be more creative and careful in leading my children. Why? Because I know I am bound to these people forever by my blood. This thought alone reminds me to treat them with the greatest respect and love, even when I know we'll need to have hard conversations at times.

> Our spiritual family bears a weight of responsibility that requires us to treat one another as family.

But there's a sense in which God's spiritual family sometimes takes precedence over even my blood. As a spiritual leader in my home, I am reminded daily that Jesus's blood joins me in my relationship with my wife and children in a way that is greater than natural relationships, because it's supernatural and spiritual. Therefore, I must treat fellow believers as brothers and sisters in Christ. And this spiritual family bears responsibility that is mine to steward as a spiritual leader every day.

So here's a question for you today: Is there a brother or sister in Christ whom you need to think about and treat differently today?

ASK THIS

Is there a follower you need to treat a little differently today?

DO THIS

Think about them as family and lead them differently.

PRAY THIS

God, may I see your children as my real brothers and sisters in Christ.

JOURNAL

SEE BELIEVERS AS FAMILY

_____

_____

_____

_____

_____

_____

_____

_____

_____

_____

_____

_____

_____

_____

_____

_____

_____

_____

_____

_____

_____

_____

_____

_____

_____

_____

MUZZLE ONCE OR HONOR TWICE

"Let the elders who rule well be considered worthy
of double honor, especially those who labor in
preaching and teaching. For the Scripture says,
'You shall not muzzle an ox when it treads out the
grain,' and, 'The laborer deserves his wages.'"

1 Timothy 5:17–18

In Jewish culture, the firstborn son received a double portion of his father's inheritance at his death. What we read here is probably an allusion to this. The text here says the pastor who teaches is deserving of double honor. This person is owed both esteem and compensation.

I love the word picture of a muzzled ox. Why is this important? Because in Deuteronomy 25:4, God established a law for how farmers leveraged animals for their advantage. He understood that some people would abuse the rights of animals by working them to death. He knew that the farmers would become so selfish that they would muzzle the animals so they could not slow down even for a snack in the field.

Many pastors feel this way. They feel overworked and underappreciated. They feel like muzzled oxen being commanded to put their heads down, keep their mouths shut, and work harder. That's quite an image now, isn't it? If you don't believe this is true, think about it for a few seconds. Recall how many critical statements you've made about your pastors this year, and weigh that against how many times you have told them you appreciate all the hard work they do for you. Does the scale tilt heavily in one direction?

So do me a favor today: tell your pastor thank you. Just a note or text is all that is needed. Let's bombard them with the honor they deserve. And if you want to double it up, pair it with a generous donation or gift card. They will love it. It happens less often than you think.

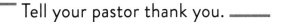 Tell your pastor thank you. ———

ASK THIS
What's the name of the pastor you need to thank?

DO THIS
Tell them thanks and double it up.

PRAY THIS
God, thank you for the many pastors who have added so much value to my life.

JOURNAL

MUZZLE ONCE OR HONOR TWICE

WORKING FOR BELIEVING
AND UNBELIEVING BOSSES

"Let all who are under a yoke as bondservants regard
their own masters as worthy of all honor, so that the
name of God and the teaching may not be reviled.
Those who have believing masters must not be
disrespectful on the ground that they are brothers;
rather they must serve all the better since those who
benefit by their good service are believers and beloved."

1 Timothy 6:1–2

The gospel has always carried a special appeal to a poorer segment of society. But in Ephesus, there weren't just poor people; the city also had a large population of the ultra-rich. This means that in the church at Ephesus, they had some members who were rich (including slave owners) and other members who were poor (including slaves)—who would worship together.

This unique socioeconomic dynamic was an area of concern for Paul, so he addressed that tension in the letter. This is what good leaders do: they tackle potential issues before they become actual issues.

The direction Paul gave here has incredible marketplace applications for a believing employee too. If we apply his direction to our modern context, we will learn a lot about how believing employees should interact in the marketplace with two types of bosses.

First, Paul spoke to the issue of a believer working under the direction of an unbelieving boss. He said that we are to think about such bosses honorably. Now occasionally, this can be a problem for believers who work for bosses who do not believe in God. But as Paul stated here, we must take responsibility for addressing any of our bad thinking that would result in dishonor.

Good leaders tackle potential issues before they become actual issues.

From time to time, unbelieving bosses are likely to do less than honorable things. But we must trust that these things will be exposed in God's time. Until then, it is our responsibility to steward how we think about our unbelieving bosses because God may use these events to drive them to him. Thus, Paul said we must always be ready by acting honorably so that when this time comes, we will bring positive attention to God's name instead of discrediting it. Now that's some incredible advice.

Second, Paul spoke to the issue of a believer working under the direction of a believing boss. Here, we assume that these bosses might go to church with them. The predicament in this situation is that believers who are employees might try to take advantage of the relationship or generosity of their believing bosses and use it as leverage or permission. Instead, Paul shouted, "No, don't do that!" He commanded them not to be disrespectful. Then he declared that this is an incredible opportunity for two believing people to serve "all the better" because they share common values and a common end.

This scenario is synergy at its best. It's the combination of believers working together in ministry using their time, talents, and treasures for the greater impact of the kingdom. I believe godly men search for experiences like this. And guess what? We can do this apart from each other, but if we do it together, something incredible happens.

At work today, work well. And if you are going to work for believers, then let's work "all the better."

ASK THIS

What work situation do you need to address today?

DO THIS

Work better.

PRAY THIS

God, help me to be the best believing employee I can be for your glory.

JOURNAL
WORKING FOR BELIEVING AND UNBELIEVING BOSSES

THREE SIGNS OF INACCURATE TEACHERS

"Teach and urge these things. If anyone teaches a
different doctrine and does not agree with the sound
words of our Lord Jesus Christ and the teaching that
accords with godliness, he is puffed up with conceit
and understands nothing. He has an unhealthy
craving for controversy and for quarrels about words,
which produce envy, dissension, slander, evil
suspicions, and constant friction among people who
are depraved in mind and deprived of the truth,
imagining that godliness is a means of gain."

1 Timothy 6:2–5

At this point, Paul began the conclusion of his letter to Timothy. It's going to feel like he just threw a bunch of random thoughts at Timothy. But he didn't. He repeated, reminded, and reiterated everything he had already stated.

Which, by the way, is what good mentors do. Saying something once is never enough. I need reminders too. I like it when people repeat and reiterate. When I am in the gym, I want to be reminded when my lift doesn't look right. When I am not performing in my job, I like to be reminded about the goal we are trying to hit. When I get lazy in my leadership as a father, I want to be reminded to step up. Why? Because these promptings help me perform and lead better.

Good mentors know that saying something once is never enough.

The predominant item on Paul's mind as a mentor was the inaccurate teaching in Ephesus. His letter began and ended with that topic. He wanted Timothy to get into the church in Ephesus and counteract this bad teaching with good teaching that agreed with the things Jesus spoke.

Then Paul dropped in three signs, or indicators, of an inaccurate teacher. They are all found in verse 4:

- Inaccurate teachers are arrogant.
- Inaccurate teachers spew senseless ideologies.
- Inaccurate teachers argue using meaningless words and terms.

Does this sound familiar? It should. This is exactly what is happening in the world across the political spectrum. It's happening today at an unstoppable rate. And it is finding its way into every institution, including churches, and people are buying into it.

So the call to action from this is twofold. First, we must be on the lookout for arrogant people (including people we might otherwise agree with) who spew senseless ideas from made-up terminology. Second, we must counter this with teaching based on the accurate and sensible teaching of Jesus Christ. Which assumes four things:

- We are getting the truth from the Book of Truth.
- We are actively discerning truth from untruth.
- We are applying truth to our lives.
- We are countering untruths by teaching the truth.

So let's be people of the truth who live by the truth, discern the truth, and tell the truth, and not be proud people who spew senseless ideologies from made-up terminologies.

ASK THIS
What do you need to do differently?

DO THIS
Share that in the following journal space.

PRAY THIS
God, convict me of the truth so I can speak and live the truth.

JOURNAL

THREE SIGNS OF INACCURATE TEACHERS

_____

_____

_____

_____

_____

_____

_____

_____

_____

_____

_____

_____

_____

_____

_____

_____

_____

_____

_____

_____

_____

_____

_____

_____

_____

_____

THE PROBLEM OF
POSITIVE GAINS

"But godliness with contentment is great gain, for we
brought nothing into the world, and we cannot take
anything out of the world. But if we have food and
clothing, with these we will be content."

1 Timothy 6:6–8

The point Paul made in these verses is essential for every believer, especially new believers. If we misunderstand what Paul said here, we will
misunderstand godly motivation. That's always something God is concerned about—our motivations, our intentions, and our desires.

The primary challenge with godliness is that it brings gain. The gain
is the spiritual fruit we discover in our relationship with God. The gain is
God and his godliness. Sometimes, the virtue of his godliness in our lives
will have personal gains, popularity gains, or profit gains as well.

But if we get distracted by these lesser gains, our motivation will get
out of alignment. Because guess what? Godliness doesn't always have a
personal gain, popularity gain, or profit gain. In fact, godliness sometimes has a *persecution* gain.

So we have to monitor the motivation behind our gains. And the way we monitor them is found in one word: *contentment.* Contentment is the barometer for our motivation. Contentment is also the regulator for training our gains.

Godliness doesn't always have a personal gain, popularity gain, or profit gain.

This leads me to a question: Is there an area of your life where you need contentment? Name it. Monitor it. And then train those gains with contentment. Remember that the only thing you truly need, Jesus, has already been gained.

ASK THIS

Is there an area of your life where you need contentment?

DO THIS

Name it and train it.

PRAY THIS

God, train my gains to only need you and nothing else. I am ready to learn contentment.

JOURNAL

THE PROBLEM OF POSITIVE GAINS

DIVERTING THE DEADLY
PROGRESSION OF SIN

"But those who desire to be rich fall into temptation,
into a snare, into many senseless and harmful desires
that plunge people into ruin and destruction. For the
love of money is a root of all kinds of evils. It is through
this craving that some have wandered away from the
faith and pierced themselves with many pangs."

1 Timothy 6:9–10

As we've seen, Ephesus was a city with a high percentage of wealthy people. So as Paul brought his letter to a close, he gave Timothy some wisdom on issues that rich people might encounter, issues that Timothy would have to watch out for.

Paul stated three progressive pitfalls that rich people fall into. First, they fixate on an object. Second, they get entangled in the desire for this object. Third, they get trapped by this desire and are destroyed by it. What's fascinating is that this is true not only with wealth but with anything we tend to overdo. It's true with food, social platforms, news media, success, material items, sports, and fitness. Mankind can take any good thing and get sucked in by the desire for it and then become trapped in sin.

But this issue arises from inside a man. It's an issue with our desires. We have an unhealthy craving for more. Our desires lure us in with an object or an idea. And while the object or idea might be good, it's our private cravings that turn our actions in a bad direction.

This is where we must attack the issue before the issue becomes an issue. We must get honest with ourselves about the desires we have. We need to play the tape forward when these rise in us. We need to look ahead to what the result of each desire will be. We should be attentive to what we covet so we can kill the harmful desires before we get entangled. Which, by the way, is precisely what Paul did here with Timothy. He was teaching him how to notice an issue before it would become an issue in the church.

Mankind can take any good thing and get sucked in by the desire for it and then become trapped in sin.

The best part about this is that believers have the power to avoid the snare of this progressive process. The Spirit, if we allow him to, will convict and redirect our every wrong desire. If we get honest with ourselves and become more sensitive to the Spirit's leading, we can turn from these desires before they become sin or even perpetual sin.

And guess what? God does this work within us. This is the battle no one ever sees and the victory many followers fail to enjoy. It's the personal conviction of the Spirit, killing the desires of sin in a man for God's glory. There is nothing like it, because it has nothing to do with you and everything to do with God's victory over your desires.

So get out there today and live in this victory. Crave the Spirit and nothing else, and you will not get dragged away from the faith with many pangs.

ASK THIS

What desire do you need to address? If you don't know right now, think more about it.

DO THIS

Ask the Spirit to kill that desire before it kills you.

PRAY THIS

God, may the Spirit you have given me be strong in me and convict me of sin before I sin.

JOURNAL

DIVERTING THE DEADLY PROGRESSION OF SIN

_____

_____

_____

_____

_____

_____

_____

_____

_____

_____

_____

_____

_____

_____

_____

_____

_____

_____

_____

_____

_____

_____

_____

_____

_____

_____

_____

SIX HIGH-SPEED PURSUITS
OF GODLY MEN

"But as for you, O man of God, flee these things.
Pursue righteousness, godliness, faith, love,
steadfastness, gentleness."

1 Timothy 6:11

Paul had just told Timothy to watch out for teachers who desired deceptive gains. Now he commanded him to run from these people and their teaching. Then Paul added a counteraction. It was a command not only to flee from bad action, bad people, and bad teaching but also to pursue good action.

I think many believers get this wrong. They try to merely stop something without starting something new. This is important because desires never remain in a neutral state. If you want to stop doing something, you must run from it and start running to something else. It's a stop and a start. It's a fleeing and a pursuing.

I think of it as two cars passing each other on a narrow stretch of road traveling at sixty miles per hour. We must flee from one thing at sixty miles per hour and pursue another thing at sixty miles per hour. But as we pass, we increase our distance from each other at a hundred twenty miles per hour. That thing in the rearview mirror is getting farther from us at twice the speed we're going because we're pursuing something new.

> If you want to stop doing something, you must run from it and start running to something else.

Paul told Timothy to pursue six things:

1. Righteousness, which I define as proper conduct toward people.
2. Godliness, obedience to God.
3. Faith, complete trust in God.
4. Love, benevolence toward people.
5. Steadfastness, staying power.
6. Gentleness, being mild in manner.

Maybe there is something you need to stop doing. Flee from it. At the same time, consider whether there is something on that list you need to start doing. If so, pursue it. And in doing so, you will watch your wrong desires fall away at twice the speed.

ASK THIS

What do you need to stop doing, and what can you start doing?

DO THIS

Share these things, and pursue what you'd like to start doing.

PRAY THIS

God, increase my distance at twice the speed. Receive my fleeing and pursuit as a sacrifice to you.

JOURNAL

SIX HIGH-SPEED PURSUITS OF GODLY MEN

LIVE IT OUT

"I charge you in the presence of God, who gives life to all things, and of Christ Jesus, who in his testimony before Pontius Pilate made the good confession."

1 Timothy 6:13

At this moment, Paul was giving Timothy a charge that is given to all believers. It's a charge to live out our confession before those who will oppose us, in the sight of God and all his creation.

In my opinion, this is the hardest thing about being a Christian: living out personal convictions in the public arena. Learning how to go public with our faith in a way that clarifies sin, elevates salvation, and brings glory to God rather than attention to ourselves. We learn to make this confession before believers by declaring Jesus as our Savior and Lord.

But this is only the first of many confessions we will have to make in this lifetime. We must now make daily confessions to believers and the world. And this is where our faith and confession are tested: with those who do not share our faith in Jesus. I believe each of us will have a moment when we stand before great opponents—our own Pontius Pilates. This will be our moment in the arena.

In my opinion, this is the hardest
thing about being a Christian:
living out personal convictions
in the public arena. _____

Are you ready? How are you faring in the public confession of your faith? How about with friends, family members, peers, or professionals who do not share your same faith in Jesus? Consider it. How are you faring?

If you are not sure, do me a favor: Get in the arena today. Confess your faith in one small way today—just one time. And maybe you'll discover Paul was right to charge Timothy to step into the arena before the presence of God, who gives life to all things.

ASK THIS

So, how are you faring in the public confession of your faith?

DO THIS

Get in the arena today.

PRAY THIS

God, give me the courage to step into the arena today. Prepare me for my moment!

JOURNAL

LIVE IT OUT

A COVENANT BETWEEN MEN

"To keep the commandment unstained and free from
reproach until the appearing of our Lord Jesus Christ."
1 Timothy 6:14

What "commandment" did Paul refer to here? The Great Commandment? One of the Ten Commandments? Or was it some private agreement that he and Timothy might have made?

I think this was most likely the *instruction* that Paul had just given to Timothy: that he needed to get in the arena and keep up the good fight.

But Paul turned this commandment into something more significant: a spiritual covenant between two men. I love this. He did something that spiritual brothers rarely do, something that needs to be resurrected: he made a spiritual covenant with Timothy. It even had declared goals and terms. The goals were:

- Remain unaffected by the heretics and their teachings.
- Remain free from public ridicule in how and what he proclaimed about Jesus.

As for the terms: this covenant is to remain in effect until Jesus comes again.

I wish we did this more often. This is positive spiritual reinforcement. It's much better than negative spiritual reinforcement or reactive approaches to spiritual growth.

> Paul did something that spiritual brothers rarely do, something that needs to be resurrected: he made a spiritual covenant with Timothy.

Why not try it? Try determining one spiritual goal with terms, then seal it in a covenant with a spiritual brother and see if it calls you to a higher commitment to God and each other. As you do it, fight the good fight hard, but do it without being lazy or becoming legalistic.

ASK THIS

Is there a spiritual covenant you need to make?

DO THIS

Make it with another man.

PRAY THIS

God, thank you for the covenant you make with us. Help me to be faithful to the covenants I make with others.

JOURNAL

A COVENANT BETWEEN MEN

_____

_____

_____

_____

_____

_____

_____

_____

_____

_____

_____

_____

_____

_____

_____

_____

_____

_____

_____

_____

_____

_____

_____

_____

ASCEND TO NEW HEIGHTS WITH GOD

"He who is the blessed and only Sovereign, the
King of kings and Lord of lords, who alone has
immortality, who dwells in unapproachable light,
whom no one has ever seen or can see. To him be
honor and eternal dominion. Amen."

1 Timothy 6:15–16

As Paul brought this letter to Timothy to a close, he ascended to great heights with seven statements of praise to God. They included three names for God and four descriptions of God.

1. Sovereign—God of all power.
2. King—God of all people.
3. Lord—God of all authority.
4. Immortal—God is deathless and alive.
5. Unapproachable—God is unreachable even in our imagination.
6. Honor—God has the highest worth.
7. Dominion—God has power demonstrated forever.

In context, the charge was for Timothy to pursue the things of the Lord, with the understanding that the God who was described in these seven ways was watching. God is the motivation and the reason we live to pursue righteousness, godliness, faith, love, steadfastness, and gentleness.

This is precisely where followers go wrong. We get distracted by acts of self-centered disobedience or acts of self-righteous obedience. Both are signs that we have forgotten God. The first method is evident because self-centered disobedience is always easy to spot. For example, in the story of the Prodigal Son, the younger son squandered his inheritance from his father through reckless living.

The second is less obvious because self-righteous obedience is elusive and deceptive and disguises itself as righteousness yet is undergirded with malicious motives. An example of it in the Prodigal Son story is the older son, who put on a great show but sought many of the same things the younger son wanted. Through self-righteous obedience, the older son tried to earn the father's love and blessing. But the problem of both sons was that they failed to see that the father had riches that were always at their disposal. Maybe they failed to see this because they were too focused on themselves.

At the end of his letter, Paul ensured that Timothy understood that the only reason he could pursue godliness was because of God, and therefore, he should keep his eyes fixed on him. Paul wanted Timothy to work hard, fight the good fight, correct heresy, and build leaders with his eyes on the summit, where God is.

So, how are you doing with this today? Are you focused on God? Or have you been distracted for too long by self-centered and self-righteous thoughts? If so, turn your eyes to the hills. Consider where your help comes from: the God and maker of all things.

—— Work hard, fight the good fight, correct heresy, and build leaders with your eyes on the summit, where God is. ——

ASK THIS

Have you been distracted by self-centered and self-righteous thoughts?

DO THIS

Turn your eyes to God.

PRAY THIS

You are my Sovereign, King, and Lord. You are immortal and unapproachable, worthy of all honor and dominion.

JOURNAL

ASCEND TO NEW HEIGHTS WITH GOD

_____

_____

_____

_____

_____

_____

_____

_____

_____

_____

_____

_____

_____

_____

_____

_____

_____

_____

_____

_____

_____

_____

_____

BE RESOLUTE

Join **Be Resolute**, a men's ministry platform founded by author Vince Miller that provides Bible studies aimed at building better men.

Find encouragement and truth
Sign up for the men's daily devo and join thousands of men all over the world.

Invite Vince to speak at your event
Bring this dynamic and devoted author and speaker to mentor the men at your ministry conference, event, or men's retreat.

Learn more at
beresolute.org

youtube.com/@VinceLeeMiller